Wheels, wings and water

Trains

Chris Oxlade

Raintree

www.raintreepublishers.co.uk
Visit our website to find out more information about **Raintree** books.

To order:
☎ Phone 44 (0) 1865 888112
📄 Send a fax to 44 (0) 1865 314091
💻 Visit the Raintree Bookshop at **www.raintreepublishers.co.uk** to browse our catalogue and order online.

First published in Great Britain by Raintree,
Halley Court, Jordan Hill, Oxford OX2 8EJ,
part of Harcourt Education.
Raintree is a registered trademark of Harcourt
Education Ltd.

Editorial: Charlotte Guillain and Isabel Thomas
Design: Sue Emerson (HL-US) and Joanna Sapwell
(www.tipani.co.uk)
Picture Research: Maria Joannou and
Su Alexander
Production: Lorraine Hicks

Originated by Dot Gradations
Printed and bound in China by South China
Printing Company

ISBN 1 844 21374 9
07 06 05 04 03
10 9 8 7 6 5 4 3 2 1

British Library Cataloguing in Publication Data
Oxlade, Chris
Trains. – (Wheels, wings and water)
1.Railroads – Trains – Juvenile literature
I.Title
385.3'7

Acknowledgements
The publishers would like to thank the following
for permission to reproduce photographs: Ace
Photo Agency, **14, 17, 19, 21**; Collections/ Colin
Underhill, **8**; Collections/ Colin Underhill, **15**;
Collections/ Lawrence Englesberg, **6, 7**; Corbis, **20**;
Rail Images, **5**; Trip/ C Kapolka, **12, 16, 18, 11,
22**; Trip/ D Harding, **13**; Trip/ G Harris, **10**; Trip/
M Bambridge, **9**; Trip/Trip, **4**.

Cover photograph reproduced with permission of
Pictures Colour Library

Every effort has been made to contact copyright
holders of any material reproduced in this book.
Any omissions will be rectified in subsequent
printings if notice is given to the publishers.

Contents

Some words are shown in bold, **like this**.
They are explained in the glossary on page 23.

What is a train?

carriage

A train is a **vehicle** that carries people and things.

It has lots of **carriages**.

seat

passenger

Each carriage is full of seats.

The people who ride in a train are called passengers.

What kinds of train are there?

Some trains carry people between towns and cities.

They are called passenger trains.

Some trains carry parcels, or coal or **ballast**.

They are called freight trains.

What makes a train go?

electric cable

This train has an electric **motor**.

Electricity comes from the cable above the train.

This **locomotive** has a diesel engine.

This engine works like a car engine, but it is much bigger.

Where do trains go?

rail

Trains go along on railway tracks.

Each railway track has two metal rails.

flange

Train wheels roll along on top of the rails.

A **flange** stops the wheels slipping off the rails.

Who drives a train?

A train driver sits in a special cab at the front of the train.

He controls the speed of the train with a handle.

red signal

There are lights called signals on the railway.

The driver stops the train when a signal is red.

How fast do trains go?

Some trains are very fast.

This **express** train goes at 300 kilometres per hour.

speed limit sign

Trains cannot go fast all the time.

The train driver must obey the speed limit.

What trains go underground?

Underground trains go through tunnels underneath the ground.

This train is in a tunnel underneath the city streets.

This train goes through a tunnel between England and France.

The tunnel goes under the sea.

Where do trains start and stop?

platform

Trains stop at railway stations.

Passengers step on to the platform.

Trains start and finish their journeys at a terminus.

There are lots of platforms here.

Where are trains made?

Trains are made in a huge factory.

Each **carriage** starts as an empty metal shell.

Sometimes trains break down.

This mechanic is using tools to mend the train.

Train map

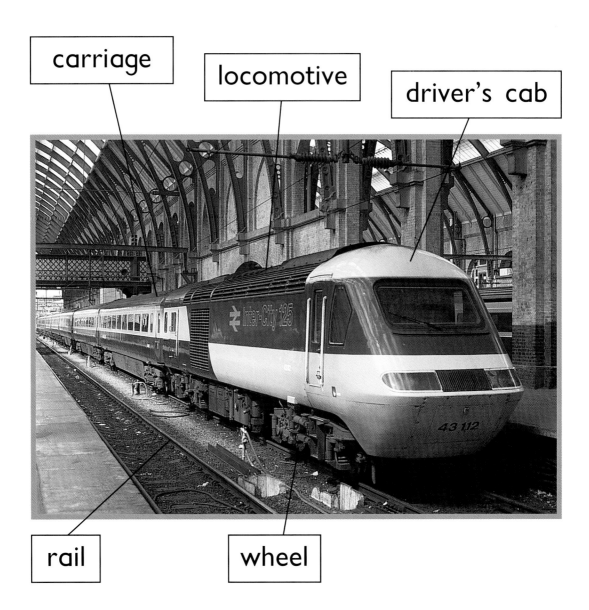

carriage

locomotive

driver's cab

rail

wheel

Glossary

ballast
small pieces of broken rock that a railway track sits on

carriage
part of a train where passengers sit, with lots of seats and windows

express
fast passenger train that only stops at big towns and cities

flange
sticking-out rim of train wheels that stop then slipping off the rail

locomotive
machine at the front of a train that pulls the carriages along

motor
machine worked by electricity that makes a vehicle move

vehicle
machine that carries people and things from place to place

Index

Titles in the Wheels, Wings and Water series include:

Hardback   1 844 21371 4

Hardback   1 844 21372 2

Hardback   1 844 21373 0

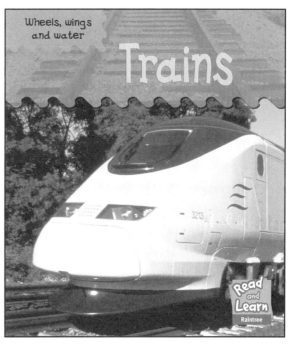

Hardback   1 844 21374 9

Find out about the other titles in this series on our website www.raintreepublishers.co.uk